THE HOW AND WHY WONDER BO

CASTLES

Written by TUDOR EDWARDS
Illustrated by EDWARD MORTELMANF

TRANSWORLD PUBLISHERS · LONDON

INTRODUCTION

We have our dream castles, and we think perhaps of that legendary castle where King Arthur and Sir Galahad walked. We think too of castles in terms of pomp and pageantry, but the reality was often much grimmer. In the Middle Ages it could truly be said that the Englishman's home was his castle, but he was likely to be starved or burned out of it. It was a time of war, when ambitious rival barons competed for royal favours and the people were often in rebellion.

There were castles or some sort of fortifications in the Mediterranean countries and the Middle East at the dawn of history. The *How and Why Wonder Book of Castles* reveals what manner of fortresses they were, and how the Crusaders brought back some of their secrets. It shows how castles developed from the simple Saxon mound to the mighty fortresses built by King Edward I to hold the people beyond the borders in check.

The book shows the important part played by castles in the Wars of the Roses and the Civil War, and in the bitter struggles which ultimately led to the amalgamation of Scotland and Wales with England. It shows too how weapons improved and how the invention of gunpowder rendered the castles obsolete. It shows how the Order of the Garter was established at Windsor Castle. It can thus be read as *history*. It illustrates architectural development and artistic expression in conjunction with military needs and can thus be read as *art*. It gives glimpses of famous statesmen and warriors in critical periods of their lives and can thus be read as *biography*. Finally it is a portrait of how people lived in war and peace, in one of the most violent but in many ways fascinating periods of our past.

Originally published in Great Britain
by Transworld Publishers Ltd.

PRINTING HISTORY
Transworld edition published 1971
Transworld edition reprinted 1972
Transworld edition reprinted 1974 (twice)
Transworld edition reprinted 1976

The How and Why Wonder Book Series is originated
and published in the U.S.A. by Grosset and Dunlap, Inc.
a National General Company.
Published by Transworld Publishers Ltd., Century House, 61/63 Uxbridge Road, Ealing, London W5 5SA
Made and printed in Great Britain by Purnell & Sons Ltd., Paulton (Avon) and London.

CONTENTS

To keep down the English, William built castles in all the large towns and at places of military importance. The Norman Bayeux Tapestry illustrates these early castles.

What is a Castle?

You must, of course, have seen many castles, for they are dotted all over the country, mostly in ruins, perched on hill-tops but sometimes rising from the meadows. Often you have seen them in the towns which have grown up around them. The stories and ballads of Sir Walter Scott—*Ivanhoe, Peveril of the Peak, The Monastery, Marmion*—give you graphic pictures of castle life, and many films will have given you a good idea of what castles used to look like.

What exactly is a castle?

The term is deceptive, for it is applied to prehistoric camps composed of vast rings of earth banks, like the famous Maiden Castle in Dorset. Confusingly, the Romans called these camps or hill-forts *castella*. And it is applied to some very large Georgian and Victorian mansions (some of which stand on the *site* of a genuine castle) with mock parapets, with drawbridges that do not go up and portcullises that do not come down. Again, we cannot regard military blockhouses, towers and redoubts as castles since they were not designed to be lived in.

So what is a castle?

We shall be getting near a true definition if we say that a castle is a fortified dwelling intended for purposes of residence and defence. Since such a dwelling was eventually rendered useless

by the use of gunpowder and artillery it follows that the true castle belongs to a past age in history. To the Middle Ages, in fact, when the home of a noble lord was his stronghold, when Kings raised castles to subdue a rebellious people, and when the feudal lords in their baronial castles waged war against each other or against the king.

Early Castles

The idea behind a castle is as old as the hills. The art of fortification had reached a high state of development at the dawn of history. The remains of powerful military works dating from the earliest periods are to be found in Greece, Asia Minor and Egypt, at Mycenae, Troy, Babylon and Thebes, and by the second century before Christ, military architecture had become a special science with schools in important centres like Rhodes. Philo of Byzantium, who flourished about 120 B.C., wrote a treatise on fortifications which describes the art or science of castle warfare at that time and which anticipates many of the features which we see at a later date. The Romans developed this art, and after their legions had left England the inhabitants continued to defend themselves behind the Roman fortifications in London, York, Chester, Lincoln, Colchester and elsewhere.

The lawlessness and continuous strife between invading Jutes, Saxons, Angles and Danes made it necessary to provide every community with defence, and to this end "burghs" or boroughs, fortified settlements, were built in various parts of the country. From the year 910 to 924 Edward the Elder and his sister Ethelfleda, Lady of the Mercians, built over twenty such fortified towns, including Warwick, Tamworth, Stafford and Hertford.

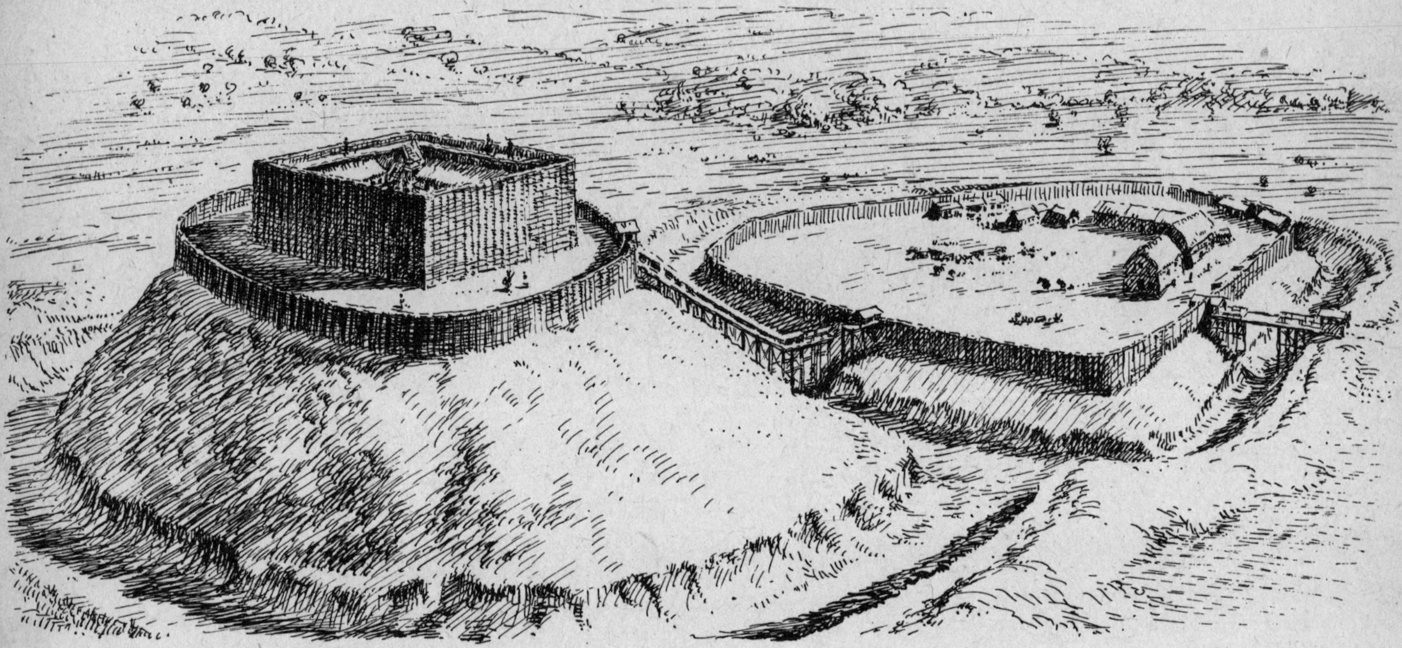

The Normans introduced the motte and bailey type of castle.

Who built the first English castles?

The castle as we know it, however, is due to the Normans, who when they conquered this country in 1066 introduced a type of fortification common in their homeland, where they were building not fortified towns but private castles. This type was the motte and bailey type, and we can see what it was like from a picture in the Bayeux Tapestry.

What is a motte and bailey?

A motte is a mound of earth, and a bailey is a ward or enclosure. The motte was usually on the edge of the bailey to enable the defenders to escape in an emergency. Wooden palisades or stockades crowned the top of the bank round the bailey and, again, round the edge of the flat top of the motte. The bailey was big enough to contain wooden buildings to house the garrison and the cattle which would be driven in to feed them during a siege. The lord's house, a tower-like structure of wood, was built on top of the motte and was connected with the bailey by a wooden bridge or gently sloping ladder across a ditch. Another wooden bridge crossed the outer ditch, which circled the whole site, to open

The first Norman castle after the defeat of Hastings.

country.

This simple form of defence was basically not so very different from the wooden settlements that the English pioneers in Canada built more than five hundred years later. There, trading posts or forts were usually established at the mouths of rivers along the coasts, and each fort consisted of a group of log cabins surrounded by high wooden stockades.

From the first moment of his landing on the English shore William the Conqueror started building his mottes and baileys on the widest scale to hold down the people. This he did in every town where he was victorious. His very first castle was at Hastings, near Senlac Hill, where he had defeated Harold and gained the English crown, and the Bayeux Tapestry shows the actual building of it. These castles were built quickly. At York a castle was ordered to be built in the summer of 1068, and it was finished and garrisoned by five hundred men before the winter. A second smaller castle in York was built in eight days!

All these early castles had wooden buildings, which were obviously unsatisfactory since they were perishable and easily destroyed by fire. Very few had, like the Tower of London, a stone keep or central tower from the beginning. But during the 12th century the owners of these first castles replaced the wooden tower with a stone keep and the wooden palisades with a low stone wall which was called a curtain. At first the keep was a type called a shell keep, which contained all the buildings of the castle placed on the inside of a large circular wall. Windsor Castle was originally of this type, and other examples include Arundel, Lewes, and Carisbrooke.

The early keep designed for living—and defence.

How did the Norman castles differ from the early models?

Then came the golden age of the Norman castle. The builders of new castles imported from the Continent the idea of a very massive square or rectangular keep with stout surrounding walls. These keeps provided well-designed and powerful dwelling-houses which were convenient and secure. They are from two to four storeys in height. The entrance doorway is usually on the second storey and is reached by a stairway built against the side of the keep. The principal hall was generally on the entrance floor. There were fireplaces, and lavatories, called garderobes, were formed in the outer walls opening up from the main rooms. There was nearly always a chapel, either in the keep itself or in a building attached to it. At Dover there is an adjoining building with two chapels, one above the other. There was always a well inside the keep. This often went down to a great depth and was carried up through two or three floors, with a place at each floor to draw the water.

Castle Rising and Kenilworth are among the finest examples of these massive square keeps. The Tower of London, perhaps the earliest and most famous of all English towers, is another brilliant example. This, of course, is the original tower, known as the White Tower, for the Tower of London ultimately consisted of many towers.

Rectangular keeps were obviously convenient for arranging the rooms inside, but they had disadvantages when the castle was being attacked, since one could not see or shoot round corners. So at the end of the 12th century the new castles had a round or polygonal keep, often called a donjon. Of this type is Conisborough in Yorkshire, one of the finest keeps in Britain, which is featured in Walter Scott's *Ivanhoe*.

Sieges

How did the castles defend themselves?

In all these castles the keep was the strongest point of resistance, but the outer curtain wall, tremendously thick, battlemented, and with loopholes just wide enough for a bow to shoot an arrow, was of greater importance. It was from the parapet of this wall that the defenders dominated the enemy outside and below. Against these solid defences the attackers could do little with their stone-throwing catapults, though the battering ram might be effective, if slow. It was more dangerous for the defenders when the enemy breached or pierced the curtain wall, dug their way up to the foot of the keep, and then worked with bore and pick against the bottom of the building to make a breach or entry.

The idea was then introduced of running projecting galleries of wood along the top of the curtain wall. There were holes in the floors of these galleries, and through them iron bolts could be shot, and stones, boiling water, hot pitch and even molten metal could be dropped on the heads of besiegers who had actually reached the wall foot. These wooden galleries were called hoardings.

Methods employed in attacking a castle.

The assailants, however, often had a more effective weapon than the bore or the ram. This was the mine. They dug trenches, and by means of a shaft they worked down until they had got below the foundations of the wall. Then they excavated a wide enough space to be filled with combustibles, which were then fired, thus making a breach in the wall. The classical instance of success in this fashion was King John's capture of Rochester Castle in 1215.

How was "the mine" used to capture a castle?

Mining was the most effective way of breaching a castle as King John proved at Rochester.

When King John refused to recognise the Magna Carta (the Great Charter of English liberty) many barons rebelled against him and waged open warfare. Rochester was held by one of these barons. The King brought up his siege engines and pounded relentlessly against the castle walls, his troops working in relays. The defenders, however, retaliated with such deadly fire that John employed miners—we would now call them sappers—to break through the curtain wall. A breach was made and the King's men broke into the bailey, where the garrison, after bitter hand-to-hand fighting, retired to the keep. The attackers then mined the keep and broke into that too. The defenders were valiant men and they compelled their assailants to retreat again and again. This siege went on for nearly three months, until the garrison had emptied their last barrel of salt beef and drained the last cask of beer. Only when it was brought to the verge of starvation did it surrender. Little mercy was shown in those days, and all the men in the castle, except the crossbow men, were ordered by King John to be hanged.

Which English castle was nearly lost to the French?

A more terrible siege was that some ten years earlier at Château Gaillard in France, on a precipitous cliff above the river Seine. Built by our Richard I during the wars with France, it was completed in 1198 and was one of the most powerful castles of the day. It has three baileys or enclosures, the inner bailey being on the edge of the cliff. The outer and middle curtain walls are strengthened by circular wall towers, and the giant donjon or round keep partly overhangs the precipice. It is roughly of the same type and date as Pembroke, but it had formidable devices that had not yet reached England. The King of France haughtily remarked to Richard, "I will take Château Gaillard if it be made of iron." To which Richard retorted, "I will hold it, were it made of butter." It was not made of butter but it nearly slipped through our fingers, for five years after it was built, in 1203, it was touch and go.

Château Gaillard was then held for King John by Roger de Lacy. The French King Philip decided to starve the English garrison into surrender, but the castle was so strong that he laid an unusual plan. He dug trenches between the river and the hill-top castle, and all round the hill, and along them at intervals he put up timber towers where he posted guards. His troops then sat back and waited for about three months. When the French had taken the town below the castle a large number of the

Despite the terrible hardships Château Gaillard managed to survive the siege.

inhabitants had been given refuge in the castle, but now, as food stocks dwindled, these people were turned out. The French troops had been ordered to allow no one to pass, and so the unfortunate townspeople were cut off between the castle and the French trenches. There they remained during a severe winter, nearly fifteen hundred of them, most of them dying from hunger and exposure. Even the stray dogs had all been eaten.

In the following spring the French began to assault the castle, and they successfully mined their way into the outer bailey. Against the outer wall of the middle bailey there was a building which contained latrines, with a chapel over them. A French soldier found the outlet of the drain from these latrines, crawled up through the drain, and reached a point just below the chapel window. Then, mounted on the shoulders of a companion, he was able to spring up to the window. With a rope he hauled up the others, and they were able to rush into the middle bailey and lower the drawbridge. The French troops swarmed over the bridge and then attempted to mine their way into the inner bailey, but the defenders counter-mined and drove them out. The wall was breached, however, and the French got into the inner court. Even then the garrison fought on, and there was no surrender.

The French had to resort to cunning to enter the castle.

The Crusaders' greatest fear was the Greek fire thrown by the Saracens.

Weapons

What are longbows and crossbows?

It is time that we looked at some of the weapons and siege engines of the Middle Ages. Among the hand weapons in use the bow and arrow was still prevalent, even long after the introduction of the crossbow. The crossbow came into prominence in European warfare early in the 12th century. It consisted of a wood stock, similar to a rifle butt, and a bow fixed to one end of the

Many different weapons were needed in castle warfare.

stock. The bowstring was stretched by means of a lever, and the bolt was released by a trigger. It inflicted terrible wounds. In open warfare the English preferred the longbow, which was about six feet long. The longbow was light while the crossbow was heavy and cumbersome. With the longbow the archer could shoot about five arrows while the crossbowman was discharging one bolt. English longbowmen were superb, and their flights of arrows broke the French again and again.

What other projectile weapons were used?

Then there were mortars called bombards, like short fat cannon, which fired large balls of stone and iron. There were various missile-throwing engines worked by springs or twisted ropes which threw huge rocks, and catapults which threw smaller stones and firebrands. Darts and poles sharpened at the ends were also thrown. Some of these projectile engines were as powerful as early cannon. At the siege of Acre in the Holy Land in 1189 one of the engines belonging to King Richard killed twelve men at one shot. Fire was also one of the chief weapons used. Flaming torches, burning pitch and boiling oil were thrown from the castle walls on the besiegers, and burning and highly inflammable missiles were projected from the engines of both sides. Greek fire, which spread in all directions, was thrown from the engines of the Saracens on the Crusaders to their great terror and consternation.

How effective were battering rams?

Scaling ladders for getting up the castle walls were frequently used, some of them being made of leather thongs so that they could be thrown over the walls. Battering rams were built within strong timber shelters like small houses, and these were protected from fire by iron plates or raw hides. They were mounted on wheels and brought up to the walls by teams of men working from the inside and propelling them along by means of poles. When in position the wheels were removed. The ram had an iron head and was swung to and fro by men working on either side. It is said that a battering ram made of twenty-three large trees and worked by about a thousand men was used to batter down the great east front of Caerphilly Castle.

What is a siege tower?

Siege towers, called beffrois (because they resembled belfries), were also built of timber, covered with raw hides and mounted on wheels. Since they were many storeys in height they enabled the attackers to fight on a level with those on the walls, or even the towers, of the castle assaulted. When brought up close enough, a bridge was thrown across from the tower to the battlements of the castle, and those in the tower rushed across it on to the walls. As we have seen, when all else failed the attackers would mine below the castle walls.

How Castles developed

How did the Crusades begin?

The Crusades were the wars undertaken by Christians against the Turks and Saracens for the recovery of the Holy Land. This means that the history of the Crusades was a long struggle for possession of the castles of Syria and Palestine. The Crusaders were astonished to find at Constantinople a double wall and ditch three miles long with a hundred flanking towers, and the outer wall was lower than the inner, so that the soldiers behind the walls of defence could all shoot at the same time at the enemy. At the sieges of Acre and Antioch the Crusaders found that they had to capture the flanking towers, which were fortresses in themselves, before they could hope to carry the walls commanded by them. Then, of course, the Crusaders themselves built such castles, like Kerak in the desert beyond Jordan and the mighty fortress of the Krak des Chevaliers in the mountains of Tripoli.

The Crusaders learned a great deal from the fortifications of Constantinople.

In the 14th century many towns developed as trading centres; centres of authority; and for defence. Most medieval towns were walled and fortified against attack.

What was the influence of the Eastern castles?

The new ideas spread very gradually through Europe from the time when, as we have seen, Richard I, with his first-hand Crusade experience, built Château Gaillard in France. Other castles in France were just as formidable. The great round keep at Coucy was the largest, strongest and most magnificent of all medieval towers. It occupied more than three times the area and was more than twice the height of the keep at Pembroke. There is a similar round tower in the town fortifications at Aigues Mortes. Aigues Mortes, Carcassonne and Avignon are the best remaining examples in France of a walled and fortified town, and Carcassonne has the double walled line of defence to be found in some of the Crusader castles. In the Middle Ages many of the towns and boroughs in western Europe were thus walled and fortified. In Britain the best preserved town walls are to be seen at York, Chester, Caernarvon and Conway.

In British castles of the 13th century the keep still retained its position as the main centre of defence, but the outer defences were strengthened. Along the straight curtain walls were built projecting towers with loopholes that looked right along the foot of the wall. A small square castle would require no more than four, one at each corner. A large castle would require not only corner towers but several intermediate ones. New castles had an outer and an inner bailey, and sometimes a middle bailey. Existing castles were added to and strengthened. We have already seen that the keep at Pembroke, with its inner bailey, was built at the end of the 12th century, but now, early in the 13th century, the castle was extended by a large outer bailey.

&W–CASTLES—SIG. B

A strong gatehouse was also a feature of the new castles. Often it had an extra outbuilding or fortification in front of it. This was called a barbican, and it limited and narrowed down the enemy's approach. The typical gatehouse of this period was that formed by two projecting circular or drum towers, guarding on each side the actual gate, which lay recessed between them. A portcullis, a heavy screen of oak and iron, could be dropped in front of the archway from a chamber above it, which contained the windlasses or pulleys or ropes to drop and draw up this portcullis. If some of the enemy got inside the long narrow passage of the barbican the portcullis would be dropped, killing some of them and trapping the others like sheep in a pen. The great Carthagenian general Hannibal was defeated by such a portcullis as long ago as 208 B.C.

Why did the barbican help fortify the castle?

The barbican was a deadly trap—even the great Hannibal was caught.

Kidwelly and Chepstow are fine examples of a typical gatehouse with drum-towers, while Pembroke and Warwick illustrate elaborate barbicans. Castle gateways reached their highest point of elaboration at Caernarvon, where there were no less than eight portcullises. There was often a drawbridge, which could also be raised and lowered by pulleys, especially where the ditch surrounding the castle had been filled with water to form a moat.

Caernarvon Castle had more portcullises than any other castle!

What living accommodation was there in the castle?

While the living apartments had earlier been contained in the limited space of the keep, it was more convenient to place them in the inner ward or bailey, either built up against the outer wall or grouped as a separate house standing within the protected area. The chief apartment was the great hall, where the lord of the castle and all his householders and retainers took their meals and spent their spare time. Many of the household slept in the hall. This hall was often, as you can see in the castles of Oakham and Winchester, a very large building divided lengthwise by rows of pillars and much resembling the nave of a church, except that if one side of it formed the curtain wall it would have arrow slits instead of windows. There are beautiful castle halls at Richmond, Leicester, Durham and Chepstow.

Here, when they were not fighting, the lords and their ladies and retainers lived quite a ceremonious life. The day was devoted to hunting and hawking, to tournaments and sports and military exercises, and in the evening, there were such games as chess, entertainments and minstrelsy. Dinner and supper were formal meals, but hospitality was lavish and there were many banquets.

Life in a castle wasn't all war.

The kitchen would be at one end of the hall. At Kidwelly there are remarkable and enormous round ovens with low vaults. At Durham the kitchen is still used to cook the meals for the students of Durham University, who eat in the great hall of the castle. At Raby Castle, also in Durham, there is a perfect kitchen filling one side of a square tower, and it has a remarkable louvre for dispelling the smoke. Perhaps the largest and most magnificent of castle kitchens is that at Alnwick, with its lofty roof of intersecting arches, where dinner has been cooked for six hundred Northumbrian stomachs.

Household accounts for the year 1265 at Odiham Castle in Hampshire give some idea of the food and drink of these times. Item: 1000 herrings 17s.; oysters 2s. 3d.; lampreys 7s. 1d. That was in Lent when no meat was allowed, but salt herrings were a staple food at all times. There is an item for one ox and a half, four pigs, four sheep, calves 21d., kids 7d. Quantities of wine drunk were small, but the supplies of beer were enormous. On April 29th 188 gallons of beer were bought, and on the following day more beer had to be brewed. The cost of beer when purchased was then a halfpenny or three farthings a gallon. There seems to have been a vast amount of salt in medieval castles, and one tower of Caerphilly Castle seems to have been filled with it.

Bedrooms would be placed in some convenient position, and indeed the position of everything would be determined by the military needs of the castle. The chapel was another important feature, and this varied in size and elaboration and position. The chapel of Ludlow Castle, now an empty shell, is a round building standing alone, the only one of its kind. It was the Crusaders who brought the round church to Britain, though only four of them have survived as parish churches. Many other buildings were ranged against the inner side of the walls—the guardrooms, soldiers' quarters, storehouses, stables and so on.

Vast stores of food, clothes and household goods were needed for the many nobles, soldiers and servants who lived in the castle.

Why were the prisons so terrifying?

Most castles had one or more prisons, usually cells in the basements of towers. They were almost always small, dark and badly ventilated. It is curious that we often call them dungeons. We read that someone was "cast into the lowest dungeon below the castle moat". This is a contradiction in terms, for the word "dungeon" is a corruption of "donjon", which was originally used for the keep or dominating tower of the castle, the highest point of a fortress in fact. The prison at Pontefract Castle in Yorkshire, where Richard II was starved to death, was 25 ft. square, and the only way in, or out, was through a hole or trap-door in the ceiling. A similar prison can be seen beneath the gatehouse of the castle of Alnwick, into which prisoners were lowered by ropes through an iron grating. The prison at Kidwelly is quite an unusual one for it is shaped like an old-fashioned bee-hive, and, again, the only way in or out was through the top. One of the most frightening of all prisons was that at Peel Castle on the Isle of Man. It was a crypt like a cavern beneath the choir of the church where the sea roared through the rocks outside and threatened to break in.

Few prisoners survived the castle dungeons.

A Look at More Castles

Why was Arundel Castle important?

Castles were nearly always built on a high commanding site or at a point where it dominated the line of communications. Arundel Castle in Sussex has been built up over the centuries into a palatial mansion, but it is easy to see why a fortress was put there in the first place. It is built upon a spur of the downs commanding the river Arun at a point where there has always been a bridge. Where there is a bridge there is a road, where there is a river there is an avenue of attack from the sea, and where the river passes through the downs there is a gap through which armies can march inland. The castle at Newcastle was placed to block the lowest ford on the Tyne river. Wallingford commanded the most important ford on the Thames. Royal castles were often built to block obvious landing places for an enemy coming from overseas—such were Dover, Hastings, and Southampton. The King also built castles in most of the towns to subdue large populations which might give trouble (they were usually *outside* the town but against the town walls).

Why were castles so numerous in Wales and Scotland?

Two areas that are thick with castles are the Welsh and the Scottish Marches or borders, for continuous warfare was waged there for centuries between English and Welsh and between English and Scots. These were obviously areas in which baronial castles supported each other, the lords uniting in common cause instead of being at each others' throats. But some of the early castles were set up in the most inaccessible places. There is William Peveril's cliff-guarded stronghold in the Derbyshire Peak (read Sir Walter Scott's *Peveril of the Peak*). And there is the legend-haunted retreat on the awesome black coastal rocks of Tintagel in Cornwall.

Where is the traditional home of King Arthur?

There is little to see in Tintagel today. When the castle was built one portion rested upon a splintered cliff standing up by the sea, the other portion

A conjectural view of Tintagel.

stood on a mainland cliff, and the two were connected by a narrow causeway. With time the causeway became a gap and then a chasm, so that the castle stands in two isolated fragments. Yet Tintagel has become a glorious place in the mind's eye, a symbol of chivalry, for it has become the mythical home of King Arthur and his knights. Here you might think of Igraine, when her husband perished in the shock of battle. You might think of the great combat waged upon the strand between Sir Marhaus, Knight of Ireland, and Sir Tristram of Lyonesse. Or you might in fancy hear the harp of Tristram in the ruined tower, and the voice of Iseult la Belle, the sad Queen of Cornwall. Did Arthur and his knights really sit grouped about a round table? Well, if you go to the great hall of Winchester Castle you will see an ancient round table, each place marked with the names of the knights, hanging on the wall.

The myth of King Arthur owes much to the medieval historian Jeoffrey of Monmouth who wrote about him as though he had lived in the 14th century. Arthur is now thought to have been a local chief living in Roman Britain. The round table may also be part of the myth.

What is a lake fortress?

Castles surrounded by marshes or muddy watercourses had the advantage of being safe against the use of mines, and in some places streams were dammed up so as to make artificial lakes. Examples of lake fortresses include the castles of Leeds (Kent), and Kenilworth (Warwickshire). In its prime Kenilworth was the greatest of all the lake fortresses, though it took shape gradually. In King John's time there was already a "pool", and in 1231 we find Henry III ordering "a fair and beautiful pleasure boat" to be moored near the door of his private chamber. He was probably responsible for the great dam that pent up the waters of brooks and created the lake of 111 acres, which was in existence in 1266.

When was Kenilworth in the hands of rebels?

The later history of Kenilworth is one of splendour, but in the Middle Ages it was a grim place. Henry III was unwise enough to present the castle to his son-in-law, Simon de Montfort, the great Earl of Leicester, who later became the King's greatest enemy. For when the King's unwise and heavy government brought about a national revolt Simon de Montfort led the barons against him. When de Montfort was about to engage the royal army on the battlefield of Evesham in 1265 (in which he was killed) his younger son, also named Simon, brought up forces to attack the King's troops in the rear. But he made the mistake of halting and camping outside Kenilworth Castle, and Prince Edward's troops fell upon him before dawn and took him by surprise. Many of Simon's men were captured in their tents, some were slain, and Simon alone managed to escape into the castle by swimming the lake in his night-shirt. A few days later came the fatal news from Evesham, and Kenilworth became the last refuge of the rebels. For six months it was besieged by the King's forces, who brought up wooden towers and siege engines to the north curtain wall and who even tried to attack in barges across the lake. In the end only starvation and sickness brought the surrender of Simon's garrison.

Simon de Montfort's son was the only survivor to escape to Kenilworth after his crushing defeat by Prince Edward.

When the Normans invaded England they also penetrated into Ireland, where they also built their castles. In the Middle Ages Ireland was under the jurisdiction of the English crown. The greatest of the royal castles were at Dublin, Trim and Drogheda. Trim Castle has ten drum towers on its walls, a square keep with two side towers, and a gatehouse and barbican. The Irish castle keeps did not conform to the English types, and as late as the 13th century they were being built as rectangles, three storeys in height, with a bold round tower at each corner.

Are there Norman castles in Ireland?

Since there was such a coming and going between castles, it follows that many of these castles were the scenes of significant historical events. We have recently had cause to remember that the first Prince of Wales was born in Caernarvon Castle. Henry V was born in Monmouth Castle. Edward II was murdered in Berkeley Castle. Richard II starved to death in Pontefract Castle. Warwick was the home of the great Earl Richard, the warrior-statesman who figures in Bernard Shaws play *St. Joan*. From Ludlow the Young Prince (Edward V and his brother Richard) set out on that unhappy journey, in 1483, which led them to a secret grave in the Tower of London. At Ludlow too Prince Arthur left his name to the north-west tower, in which he died in 1502, thereby ensuring the succession to the throne of his formidable brother, Henry VIII. Both Edward III and Henry VI were born in Windsor Castle. Windsor, of course, became the greatest of the royal castles, and it is still a royal palace.

Which castles are connected with famous historic events?

The Princes set out on their last journey.

WINDSOR CASTLE

Windsor, the seat of kings.

The Story of Windsor Castle

Why is Windsor castle so famous?

Windsor's massive round tower rises above the Thames, and we strain our eyes to see if the standard flies above it to show that the royal family is in residence. It has, in fact, been a royal residence for nearly a thousand years. William the Conqueror threw up a Norman motte and bailey castle there, and from the beginning it had two large baileys, the Upper and Lower Wards that we see today. Dividing the two baileys is the great round keep on its mound, representing the original motte. For a time it was the fortress and hunting lodge of William the Conqueror and William Rufus.

Windsor saw chivalry, art, statesmanship and romance.

The three kings Henry I, II and III built much of the early castle, enclosing it with curtain walls and adding towers and residential apartments, but it was Edward III who was responsible for much of what we see today. Here in 1328 he brought his bride Philippa of Hainault, and there were great feasts, tournaments, dances, minstrelsy and jousts or duels on horseback. This chivalrous if somewhat showy monarch made the castle his favourite residence, and one of his chaplains was William of Wykham, who became the great building-bishop of Winchester.

What is the Order of the Garter?

Edward had the idea of building a large round hall to house a "Round Table" for his knights after the manner of King Arthur, but the scheme was abandoned. Instead, on St. George's Day, 1349, he established the Most Noble Order of the Garter, the highest order of knighthood in the world. Today the Order is still limited to a quota of twenty-four knights. The insignia or emblem is a garter, and the motto is *Honi soit qui mal y pense* (Evil to him who evil thinks). Edward built St. George's Hall and remodelled the chapel, both for his knights, and he lined the sides of the Upper Ward with handsome residential buildings. Altogether, it may be said that it was Edward III who turned Windsor from a fortress into a palace. Early in the next reign the Clerk of the Works here was no less a person than the courtier-poet, Geoffrey Chaucer, author of *The Canterbury Tales*.

When was the castle captured?

As a fortress Windsor saw very little action. A half-hearted siege by the barons who had turned against King John came to nothing. Only once was the castle captured by enemies, in 1400. Richard II had been overthrown, and his supporters hatched a plot for seizing and slaying the new king, Henry IV, who was celebrating Christmas in the castle, without his troops. Richard's followers collected four hundred lancers and pounced on Windsor before dawn. Some of their friends inside opened one of the postern gates, and they thought for a moment that they had captured the new king and all his family. But Henry had been warned by a traitor a few hours before, had taken to horse with his sons and had ridden off to London through the darkness of a winter's night. The attackers made no attempt to hold the castle, and they retreated westward. A few days later they paid the full penalty with their lives.

Who was imprisoned in Windsor castle?

The great Round Tower of Windsor was used as the castle prison almost from the time it was built until 1660. The first notable prisoner confined here was the poet-King of Scotland, James I, who was brought here as a boy He was only ten when he was on his way to France to complete his education and he was taken prisoner by the English. He was held captive here for nineteen years. During that time he used to look out from his tower prison into a garden where the beautiful Lady Jane Beaufort, daughter of the Duke of Somerset, used to walk. They fell in love, and later Lady Jane became the wife of the poet-king.

rooms, all with woodcarvings by Grinling Gibbons and ceiling paintings by Italian artists.

Who else made additions to the castle?

It was Edward IV who built the large and glorious St. George's Chapel. This is a masterpiece of Perpendicular architecture, the Tudor Gothic style of the 15th century, and it ranks second only to Westminster Abbey as a treasure house of English art. The stalls and stall plates of the Knights of the Garter are unique, and here lie the bodies of many kings—Edward IV, Henry VI, Henry VIII and Charles I, as well as kings of this century.

Gradually the buildings of Windsor piled up. Queen Elizabeth added the Long Gallery leading from the royal apartments to the descent into the Park, which now forms part of the Great Library. She was also responsible for the state beds which shine with gold and silver. In the 17th century the Merry Monarch, Charles II, found the rooms of his palace "melancholy and of a decayed magnificence". He demolished the outer walls of most of the buildings of Edward III, did away with some of the battlements, and introduced new windows and chimney-pots. Prince Rupert was then Constable of the castle, and he hid himself like a hermit in the keep, where he kept a strange library, forges and all manner of scientific instruments. It was during this period that the great architect, Sir Christopher Wren, added the Star Buildings, the grand staircase, and seventeen state

Knights of the Garter assembled in St. George's Chapel.

Windsor remained in this state until 1824, when George IV began a thorough restoration of the castle. His architect was Jeffrey Wyatt, who tried to make Windsor look like a medieval castle again, and overdid it, but he did create the splendid palace that we see today. It cost a million and a half pounds, a fabulous sum in those days, and when it was finished Jeffrey Wyatt had become Sir Jeffrey Wyatville.

The Welsh had no love for the conquering English kings.

Castles in Wales

Why was Henry II determined to subdue Wales?

It is recorded that one day as Henry II rode through some part of Wales, attended by a splendid retinue of knights and courtiers, he looked with a contemptuous eye on the Welsh gentlemen riding on their rough ponies, and on the poorer people who were clad in sheeps' or goats' skins. A mountaineer approached the great king and said proudly, "You see these poor people, but, such as they are, you shall never subdue them—that is reserved alone for God in his wrath."

For the Welsh had never been conquered, though they had been oppressed by Romans, Saxons and Normans. The Normans had managed to subdue a great part of Wales by means of their castles stretching from Chester to Chepstow. The Welsh Marches or borders were now thick with castles. Chains of castles extending to Pembroke and northward up the river valleys, from Shrewsbury into the mountains, and from Chester to Criccieth, were all block-houses to hold each new local conquest. Henry I had almost completed the conquest of Wales, but the civil wars of Stephen's reign gave the Welsh a breathing space, and the native princes organized national resistance and recovered much of their lost territory. Henry II was forced to abandon his hopes of conquest and be content with a kind of vassalage.

The Welsh princes had their own castles. In North Wales there was Dolwyddelan, which copied the English rectangular keep and was probably the birthplace of Llewelyn the Great, the Lord of Snowdon, whose raiding parties gave the English so much trouble. Dolbadarn commanded the northern entrance to the mountain pass of Llanberis. Dinas Bran (the Hill of the Crow) dominated the valleys which come down to the river Dee near Llangollen. Powys Castle, near Welshpool, was known as Castell Coch (the Red Castle). Llewelyn the Great and his grandson built a group of stout castles which included Ewloe, which challenged the power of the English Earl of Chester.

King Edward I, who had been so victorious in the Crusades and in France, strongly believed that England would not become one of the greatest nations until the whole island of Britain was one. He vowed to finally conquer Wales and Scotland, which had long opposed the English crown. In 1282 Llewelyn, grandson of Llewelyn the Great, was drawn into a final battle with Edward, and at Builth in the Wye valley he was slain. His brother David, his wife and children were carried in chains to the castle of Rhuddlan, and David was hanged, drawn and quartered.

What are the advantages of a concentric castle?

To maintain his final conquest of Wales Edward I, in the last twenty years of the 13th century and the early years of the next century, built a series of castles in the north which represented the high watermark in medieval fortification. His concentric castle was the last word in castle building. It was called "concentric" because each ward was wholly contained within that outside it. In other words there were two or three rings of walls one inside the other. Each defensive wall was strongly fortified by towers placed astride it, and the inner walls were raised in height. These wall towers were each as strong as the old keep and could be separately defended, so that in the new castles a keep was not necessary. These castles are sometimes called "Edwardian", but this is not really a suitable term because Caerphilly in South Wales, the model of them all, was built not by Edward but by the Earl of Gloucester in 1267.

The ruins of Caerphilly are vast and still imposing. When Lord Tennyson visited them he exclaimed, "It is not a castle; it is a town in ruins." In its prime it rose from a great artificial lake. Its outer wall had a semi-circular bastion at each corner, and it had two strong gatehouses. The inner wall was much higher, with an even higher circular tower at each corner, and two gatehouses to match those in the outer wall. The inner ward or bailey was a magnificent pile of buildings with a beautiful great hall. But

Edward I was given the excuse to start the conquest of Wales when Llewellyn, the Welsh Prince and vassal to Edward, refused to do homage. The Welsh taught him some military lessons, but strength prevailed in the end.

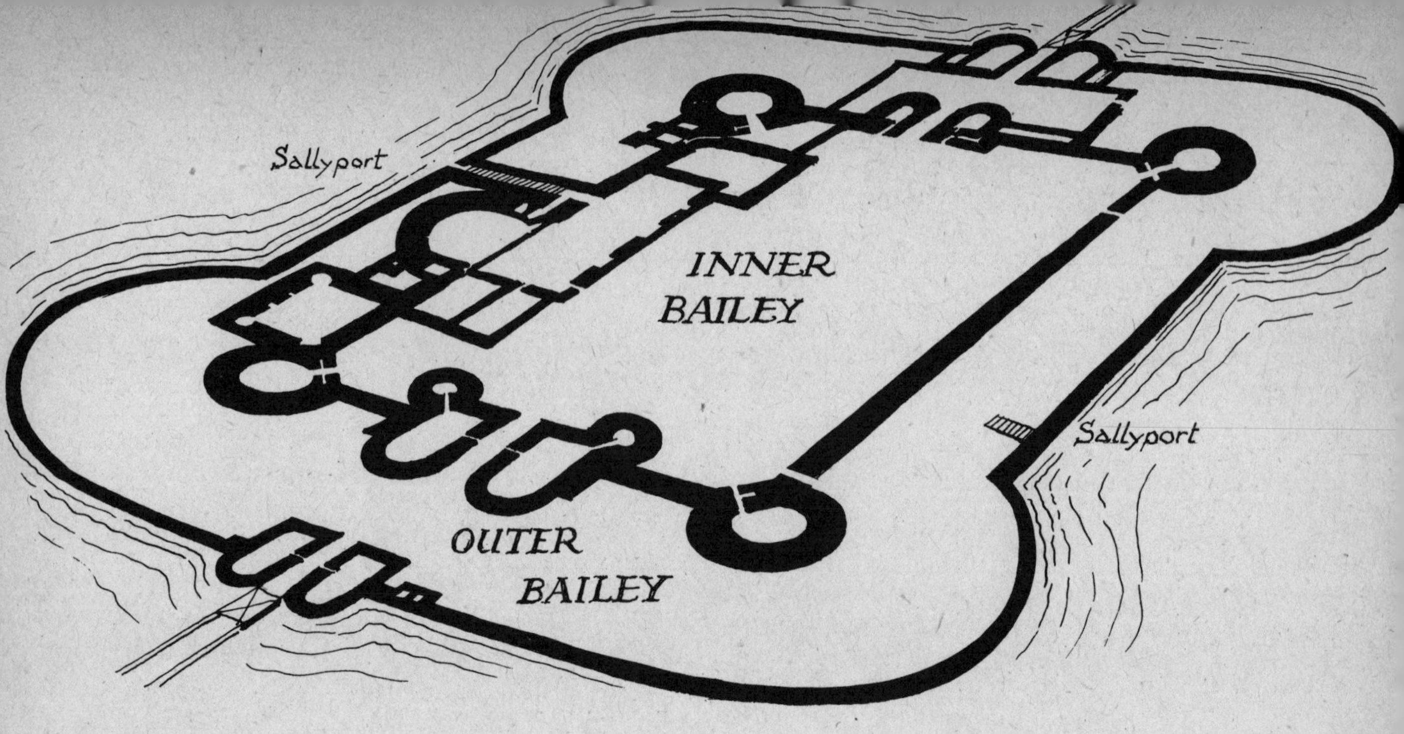

The castle reached the peak of its development in the concentric castles of Edward I

the special feature of Caerphilly was that outside the island fortress it had a vast fore-building or screen, with a powerful barbican, covering the east front, with yet more defensive works on the north.

Who was Master James of St. George?

These new castles were the products of English wartime experience in the Holy Land and France. Edward employed as his architect a man with the high-sounding name of Master James of St. George, but little is known of him except that he came from Savoy in France and was master of the royal works in Wales, drawing at one period a salary of three shillings a day in the money of that time, and later a yearly retaining fee of one hundred marks. We know that he worked on Rhuddlan, Conway, Harlech and Beaumaris.

The first of Edward's new castles was the rebuilding of Rhuddlan, begun in 1277. It is an imposing example of a concentric castle of simple design. In the same year Flint Castle was begun, and it was planned with the town as a single composition like the French *bastide*. Its most remarkable feature is the great round tower, which is mentioned in Shakespeare's *Richard II*. This great circular keep was set outside one corner of the castle, to which it was connected by a drawbridge. After yet another Welsh uprising Denbigh Castle was strengthened, and here the most important feature is the powerful triangular gatehouse with three polygonal towers. The fine archway is surmounted by a sculptured figure which is thought to be that of King Edward I (as at Caernarvon). As at Flint, Conway, Caernarvon and Beaumaris, the castle had a walled borough dependent on it.

Harlech Castle stands boldly upon a high rock, with a piece of land separating it from the sea. It is a rectangular

The Welsh castle of the "Men of Harlech".

castle and has two lines of walls forming inner and outer baileys, with an outer bailey which extends down the precipitous slopes of the hill. The main gatehouse was the stronghold of Harlech, for it had a barbican with three gates and three portcullises. The gatehouse still has its three floors, containing the private dwelling rooms of the Constable, two private chapels and guardrooms.

Two of the greatest of the new castles were Conway and Caernarvon, and though they are not strictly concentric in plan concentric principles are embodied. Conway closed the approach to Snowdonia by land and river. It was roughly oblong in plan and was divided into two wards by a thick wall. There was no gatehouse, but the approach from the walled town led through an outer gate up a steep ascent, over a drawbridge thrown across the ditch separating town from castle, and then through a barbican and inner gate. With its eight round towers Conway looks the ideal medieval castle.

What is Caernarvon's history?

Caernarvon was the most important of the Edwardian castles, and from 1284 to 1536 it was the administrative centre of Wales. The castle was built over three main periods, or in three stages. Begun in 1285, it was not finished until 1322. In shape it is like an hour-glass, with the two wards almost coming together in the middle, and it has polygonal towers at each angle. The Eagle Tower is one of the largest single towers built in the Middle Ages, and it has many of the elements of a keep. The lofty curtain walls have, on one side, two tiers of mural or wall passages containing loopholes so that, including those on the battlements, there would be three tiers of armed men. There are two gatehouses and nine wall towers, many of them having turrets as at Conway. Altogether the castle would be bristling with archers standing at different levels. On one side the castle is washed by the waters of the estuary, and the waters were diverted to form a moat on the other side, though this moat is now filled in and paved over. Caernarvon ranks among the finest examples of medieval military art, and its curtain walls and towers stand intact, though the great hall has been destroyed. The town walls too are almost intact. Nowhere in Britain can you see the full lay-out of a medieval town and castle as at Caernarvon and Conway.

King Edward's son, the first English Prince of Wales, is traditionally supposed to have been born in the Eagle

Edward I showed respect for Welsh sentiment by keeping the core of the principality intact. Parts of the Welsh law were retained, and the King's son was made Prince of Wales. Following this tradition, Prince Charles was invested as Prince of Wales in 1970.

Tower, and his presentation to the Welsh people was recently commemorated there in the ceremonial investiture by Queen Elizabeth II of her son, Charles, as Prince of Wales.

The history of Caernarvon was very much the history of Conway. In 1295, when the building of Caernarvon was half finished, another descendant of Llewelyn roused the people to rebellion when a large crowd was in the town for a fair. The castle was taken, and the Constable was hanged, and King Edward hurried into the town for the last time. He was forced to retreat to Conway, after losing his baggage train, and there he was dangerously besieged, for a high tide prevented the boats containing his supplies from crossing the river. He was able to put down the rebellion within a year, but he was forced to rebuild Caernarvon.

Owen Glendower

After Edward I had taken over Wales and built his mighty fortresses to subdue the people, life was very different for the oppressed inhabitants. The little Welsh farmer came fearfully to the strange walled town bristling with towers, driving his cattle before him or carrying his bundles of fresh farm produce. In his ignorance of the new market regulations he would commit some petty offence and be hauled off to the prison. The people grumbled and muttered oaths against the English, and bands of rebels hid in the mountains and did all they could to annoy the "foreign" authorities.

Edward I introduced the English law and administration of justice to secure order in Wales. Many Welshmen were confused by these changes and fell foul of their conquerors.

Episodes in the life of Owen Glendower, the last great Welsh leader.

Who led the last Welsh rebellion?

There was one among them who became their leader. His name was Owen Glendower. He was high-born and was descended from Llewelyn, last Prince of Wales. Although he had been attached to the household of Richard II in London, a passionate love for Wales burned in his breast, and his resentment against the English smouldered into hatred. He returned to Wales, and in the mountain glens he drilled his recruits and made an army out of raw farm lads.

Towards the close of the 14th century Owen began his rebellion, and with a great force of men he attacked the King's castles. He burned down the cathedrals at Bangor and St. Asaph because the bishops were loyal to the King, he ruthlessly sacked the property of royalist sympathisers, and in the valleys he destroyed everything that might aid the King's troops. The English, of course, also laid the land waste, so that the valleys of the north became so desolate that it was said that grass grew in the market place of Llanrwst and deer fed in the churchyard.

This great Welsh patriot, whom Shakespeare referred to as one who was "not in the role of common men", had qualities of statesmanship, for he was the first to petition for a Welsh University, and his assemblies were remarkable meetings that resembled later parliaments. Yet he often brought misery upon his own people by his actions and by the reprisals which they drew from the English.

When did Wales almost achieve its independence?

In 1400 Owen Glendower, at Machynlleth, styled himself King of Wales. His army swept through the land with a fierce determination to break every kind of royal and baronial power. Marching through South Wales they laid waste every enemy castle, Montgomery, Radnor, Carmarthen, Dynevor, Caer Cynan and many others.

At Radnor they beheaded the entire garrison. When they reached Cardiff they destroyed the town because of its royalist sympathies, but one street was spared because a friendly Franciscan monastery stood there. From Cardiff they marched to Caerphilly and laid siege to the castle. Edward hurriedly sent the Duke of York with nine hundred spear men and archers and a force of Devon men. History is rather vague about the outcome of all this, but it appears that Owen won the day, and that his men held the castle for nearly four years while he pursued his war in the rest of Wales.

One day, so says an old story, while living with his poet friend, Rhys Goch, on the banks of the Nantmor river, Owen was surprised by the followers of a neighbouring hostile squire. He and his friend fled disguised as serving men, and then separated. Owen swam the tidal river and then climbed a steep mountain peak where none dared follow him. Near there he lived in a cave for six months, a monk of a nearby monastery supplying him with food.

Where was the last Welsh stronghold?

At one time he took the castle of Conway, but he was beaten off by Caernarvon's eighty archers. In 1404, after a siege of many months he captured the impregnable castle of Harlech, for the English garrison had been reduced by sickness and starvation to twenty-one men. Owen then made Harlech his main arsenal and storehouse for weapons and provisions, and there also for safe keeping he placed his wife, daughter and grandchildren. When Owen was defeated in the open field, the castle was held by his father-in-law, Edmund Mortimer. The English besieged it for eight long months, and when Mortimer died of exhaustion the rest of the rebels surrendered. Owen's wife, daughter and the children were sent to London, but his wife and the children died within a few months of their long ordeal. In the following year Owen's army in South Wales was completely destroyed before Grosmont Castle by Prince Henry.

When the great Welsh rebellion finally died away in failure, Owen disappeared forever into the misty solitude of the mountains. His revolt was really ill-timed for Wales. The abbot of Valle Crucis Abbey was walking on the Berwyn mountains early one morning when he met Owen Glendower, now old, overthrown and dejected. "Sir Abbot", remarked Owen, "you have risen too early". "No", the abbot replied, "it is you who has risen too early—by a hundred years."

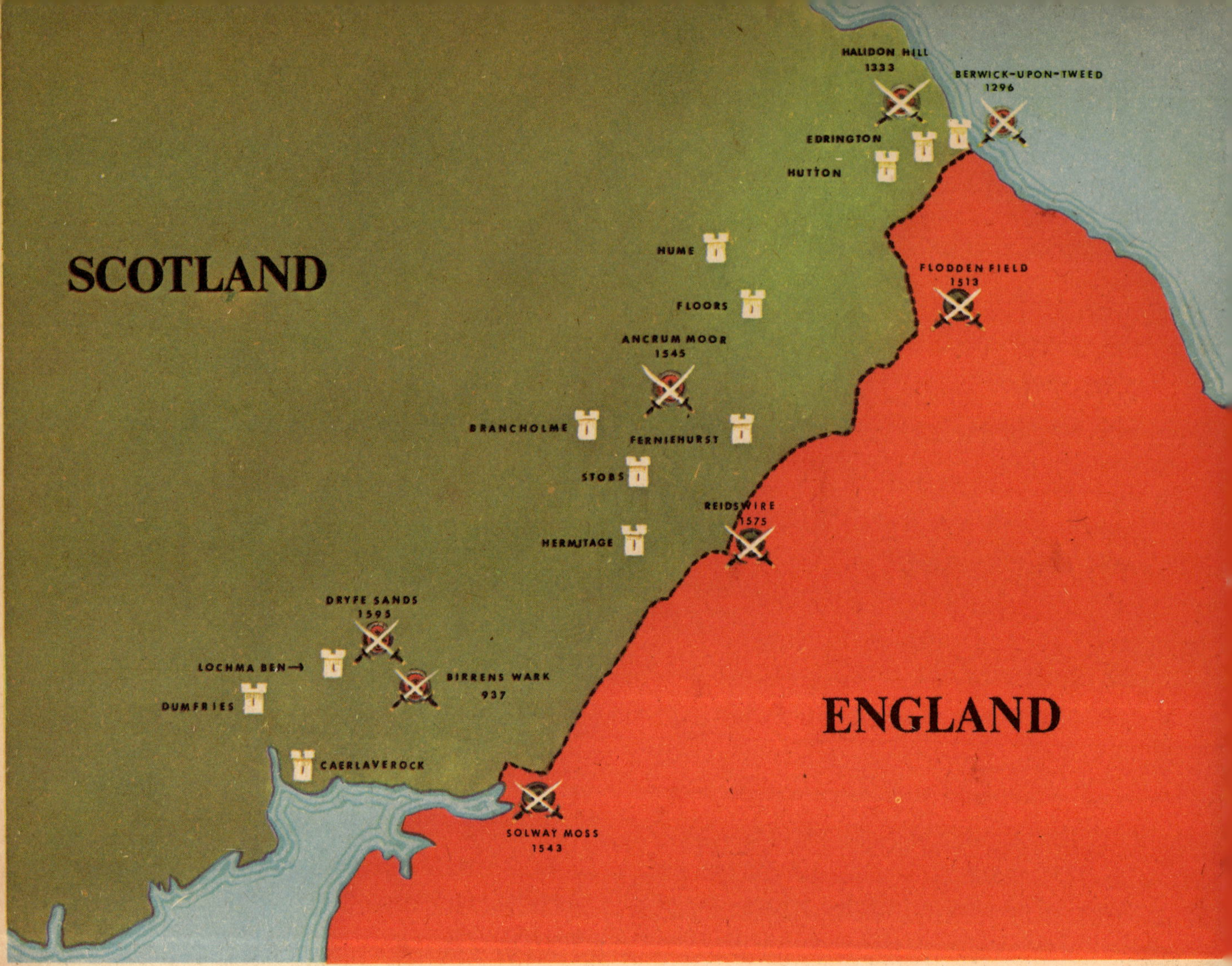

The Anglo-Scottish border, always at war, was studded with castles.

Castles of Scotland and the Border

Having conquered Wales, King Edward I attempted to conquer Scotland after two centuries of peaceful co-existence between the two countries, and there was bitter warfare for centuries afterwards. Scots raiding parties would make forays over the Border, pillaging and burning and driving English cattle back to their own lands. The English lords in their castles, which had mushroomed up all over the north, were equally savage in their treatment of the Scots. A line of strong castles belonging to the King administered by his lords, who were called Wardens, stretched across the north of England from Carlisle to Berwick-on-Tweed, through Cumberland, Westmorland and Northumberland. In addition to the many castles there were numerous strong points in the form of fortified houses known as pele towers, from the Latin word *palus*, a stake—meaning originally the early palisade.

In all the Border warfare Alnwick was one of the strongest fortresses on the English side, and it marked the downfall of two Scottish kings. Despite several rebuildings, the plan of the castle is not greatly altered, and among its impressive features is the outer gatehouse and barbican projecting near one hundred feet. It was, and is today, the seat of the Percys, now Dukes of Northumberland. They were the great enemies of the Douglas family, the leading nobles on the Scottish side of the Border. It was from Alnwick that the great Harry Hotspur sallied forth to meet the marauding force led by Douglas, who was now laying waste with fire and sword the north of England down to the gates of York. And it was almost within sight of Alnwick, on the battlefield of Otterburn, that Douglas was slain by Hotspur's own hand, though the English lost the day and Hotspur himself was taken prisoner.

What outstanding features does Alnwick possess?

The castle of Berwick was originally Scottish, but it changed hands eight or nine times between 1214 and 1482, when it was finally surrendered to the English crown. Some of its sieges were fierce and terrible, and the unsuccessful attack by Edward's forces upon the Scottish garrison in 1318 was remarkable for the unusual measures to which the English resorted. While one force attacked the castle, a large ship was towed towards the town from the mouth of the river. The ship had a boat filled with armed soldiers and drawn up mid-mast high. A kind of bridge was fixed to the bow of the boat, which was intended to drop upon the town wall, thus affording a passage from the ship into the town. The ruse failed, and the ship was burned by the Scots. Other similar desperate measures also failed.

At the siege of Berwick the English adopted desperate measures, but the Scots managed to maintain their position.

Since the Scots had their own castles, let us look at some of them. Among the most famous are Stirling, Edinburgh and Rothesay. Most of them changed hands several times during the fighting. Caerlaverock by the Solway shore is one of the rare moated triangular castles, a gatehouse flanked by drum towers at the apex, and a drum tower at each of the other two corners. Rothesay on the Isle of Bute is a moated circular castle of the early round keep type, with four stout round towers defending the circular curtain wall. This once sustained a famous siege by the Norsemen, the invaders from Scandinavia. In the reign of James IV of Scotland a barbican passage with a suite of royal apartments over it was added in front of the entrance gate.

Which Scottish castles are famous?

At Tantallon, overlooking the sea from the high cliffs of East Lothian, is one of the most imposing castles of its type in Britain. It was a seat of the Douglas family, the sworn enemies of the Percys. In *Marmion* Walter Scott writes of

His towers, Tantallon vast;
Broad, massive, high and stretching far,
And held impregnable in War,
On a projecting rock they rose.
And round three sides the ocean flows.

In plan it is a simple walled rectangle enclosing the inner bailey, with a gatehouse and, within, a single range of domestic buildings. The middle and outer baileys are formed not by walls but by moats.

What is a tower house?

In the heart of the Border country, bleak and lonely, stands the castle of Hermitage, a striking rectangular block called a "tower house", with great square wings. Mary Queen of Scots rode there and back in a day, nearly fifty miles, on a romantic visit to the wounded Earl of Bothwell. It was also Sir Walter Scott's favourite castle—he had his portrait painted with the castle as a background. The tower house was almost entirely peculiar to Scotland. It was much more of a fortified residence than the pele tower, and it resembled the ancient square keep.

Who was the Scottish patriot who routed the English?

There came a point in King Edward's campaign when he had to fight John Balliol, self-styled King of Scotland, for possession of the castle of Dunbar. Ten thousand Scots are said to have perished in the battle. Within two months all the important Scottish castles, Stirling, Edinburgh, Jedburgh, Dumbarton, Roxburgh and many others were in Edward's hands. For a time he thought he had subdued Scotland, but these proud people could not be reconciled to a "foreign" yoke. There arose a man named Wallace, the second son of the Knight of Ellerslie, who gathered the chiefs around him. They attacked the English wherever they could, taking castle after castle, and then, forty thousand strong, they appeared before the great fortress of Stirling. To oppose them, the English brought up an army

The news of Wallace's massacre of the English at Stirling Bridge aroused all Scotland. Within a few weeks the victors were raiding northern England.

of fifty thousand infantry and a thousand horsemen. The morning of September 11th, 1297, dawned on a fearful scene at the narrow Bridge of the Forth. Half the English had barely reached the Stirling bank when down rushed the Scots from the heights. The English, thrown into confusion, perished by the thousand, either on the Scottish swords or in the river. Stirling Castle was taken, and soon Edinburgh surrendered.

This state of things could not last, for the English had greater resources, and it was not long before Wallace's army was destroyed near Falkirk. The survivors fled with Wallace to Stirling, and the English went after them, to find Wallace had fled and the town burned. Wallace went back to the wild life he had known, a wandering guerrilla-chief harassing the English where he could.

Edward now besieged Stirling Castle, where the Scottish garrison was holding out, and though now an old man he directed the attack in person, even though he was struck by stones and spears from the castle and an arrow had lodged in his armour. It was a long siege, and no impression was made by the thirteen tremendous battering rams and the brass-tipped darts shot from machines. Edward grew so desperate that he wrote to the Sheriffs of London, Lincoln and York to buy up all the bows and arrows and engines of war that were to be found in their districts. After three months the castle was practically destroyed and the garrison, weary and starving, were captured, all to be sent into prison. A worse fate awaited Wallace, now imprisoned in the castle of Dumbarton, for the hope of Scotland was hanged in London. Edward's plans were still to be thwarted, however, for another Scottish leader arose. His name was Robert the Bruce.

Who learned a lesson from a spider?

In 1305 Bruce was crowned King of Scotland, but being attacked by the English he retreated to Ireland and hid on the island of Rathlyn. There he noticed a spider try six times to fix its web to a beam in the ceiling. Now shall this spider teach me what I am to do, thought Bruce, for I also have failed six times. The spider made a seventh effort and succeeded, whereupon Bruce returned to Scotland, collected three hundred followers and at midnight surprised and overwhelmed the English garrison in Turnberry Castle. In two years he made himself master of well-nigh all in Scotland, which in 1328 Edward III declared to be an independent kingdom.

Bruce learnt a lesson from the spider's determination. He steadily seized castle after castle in the lowlands and then defeated Edward II's troops at Bannockburn.

The Wars of the Roses

How did the Wars of the Roses get their name?

The failure of the English to conquer France and the unwise governing of Henry VI led to the civil conflict of the Wars of the Roses (1455–85). The direct occasion for the outbreak of this war, however, was the rivalry between the House of Lancaster and the House of York, both claimants to the throne. The emblem of the Lancastrians was a red rose, the emblem of the Yorkists a white rose. Since all the lords were divided in their allegiance it follows that their castles figured in the fighting. The decisive battles, however, were fought in the open country, and the few castle assaults and sieges were purely incidental and of little more than nuisance value.

Which was the principle Lancastrian stronghold?

In Wales the principal Yorkist stronghold was the castle of Denbigh, while Harlech was Lancastrian. After their defeats at the Battle of Towton (1461) and Bamburgh, North Wales was one of the few areas where the Lancastrians still held out. Jasper Tudor, Earl of Pembroke and half-brother of Henry VI, made Harlech his headquarters, but when things got too hot for him he fled to France. The castellan or keeper of the castle, Sir David ap Jevan ap Einion, beat off several Yorkist attacks. He is reputed to have boasted that "he had once in his youth maintained a castle in France so long that every old woman in Wales had heard of it, and in his old age he had held a castle in Wales so long that every old woman in France had heard of it". But he was finally starved into surrender, in 1468, by Edward's Welsh champion, Sir Richard Herbert. The well-known song of the "March of the Men of Harlech" is said to recall some forgotten episode of this long siege.

Harlech was the last castle surrendered to the Yorkists, and the war ended with the defeat and death of the Yorkist Richard III at the Battle of Bosworth Field. His successor, Henry VII, was descended from John of Gaunt, and he married a descendant of Edmund Langley, thus uniting the two rival Houses.

The Battle of Bosworth raged chiefly between Richard's followers, and those of Henry of Richmond. The king nearly slew Richmond with his own hand when he was overwhelmed with numbers and slain.

The Last of the Castles

Why were castles no longer built?

Few real castles were built after the close of the 14th century. Those that were, were mansions with some semblance of defence. Moat, drawbridge and battlements still appeared, but walls were thinner and windows larger. Residential comfort was the aim. Also, there was little point in building expensive defences when explosive artillery was becoming increasingly effective. Another reason was that the Tudor kings broke the power of feudalism (the system whereby the nobles held different parts of the country, for which they paid the king homage and military service). From that time any magnate wishing to fortify his house had to apply to the king for "licence to crenellate". Among the last batch of such castles to be built towards the close of the 14th century are Bolton Castle, Sheriff Hutton Castle and Snape Castle, all in Yorkshire. Bodiam Castle, in Sussex, begun in 1386, stands in a rectangular moat and has a drum tower at each corner, and a gatehouse with square towers, in which the first loopholes for the use of firearms can be seen. Bodiam looks the ideal castle.

Raglan, in Monmouthshire, started about 1465 as a great military castle and ended by being a splendid Tudor palace. It is moated and it has a great hexagonal keep, but instead of military baileys there are pleasant courts and even a bowling green. Perhaps the very last real castle to be built was at Thornbury in Gloucestershire. Edward Stafford, Duke of Buckingham, made such a stronghold of it that he was executed by Henry VIII in 1521, leaving his castle unfinished.

What were the Channel forts?

In Scotland, where the power of the Crown was weak and clan warfare persisted, castles and fortified dwellings continued to be built well into the 17th century. The royal castle of Glamis was one. There was in England, however, an isolated development for which Henry VIII was responsible. Having made enemies in Europe he feared an invasion, and he decided to build at various points along the south coast a line of forts or miniature castles, designed for artillery and equipped with the latest type of guns.

A typical coastal fort of about 1500.

These forts were built about 1500, and you can see well-preserved examples at Walmer in Kent, Camber in Sussex, and St. Mawes in Cornwall. Each is built as a compact block which could be defended all round by guns mounted on platforms rising in tiers one behind the other. For this reason they are all roughly round, with a low round tower or keep in the middle. The whole is covered by a flat roof, and, inside, a gallery pierced with numerous loopholes runs all round the outer wall.

The End of the Castles

What was the effect of the Civil War on castles?

In 1642 the Civil War broke out over the differences between Charles I and his Parliament. The supporters of the King were called Royalists (or Cavaliers), and the supporters of Parliament, led by Oliver Cromwell, were called Parliamentarians (or Roundheads). As in the Wars of the Roses, the lords and squires were divided between both sides, and each attacked the other's castles and manor houses, though the decisive battles were fought in the open country, at Marston Moor, Edgehill, Naseby and elsewhere. This time, however, far more damage was done and few castles escaped.

Why did so few castles survive?

The most epic defence of a Royalist castle was that of Corfe Castle in Dorset, held by the gallant Lady Banks in 1643. Three years later the castle was again besieged by the Parliamentarians, who gained possession of it through the treachery of an officer in the garrison. The castle was then "slighted" or blown up with gunpowder.

In Wales the last castle to hold out for the King was Harlech. The very last Royalist stronghold was Pontefract Castle in Yorkshire. Three times besieged by Cromwell's men, it never surrendered until it was starved out. This was once one of the most powerful castles in the country, and it was then known as the Troy of England. Its prison was notorious and many high-born men were executed there. It was then called Pomfret, and Pontefract is still renowned for its Pomfret Cakes made from the liquorice plant which has been cultivated there since the Middle Ages.

Up and down the country, wherever the victorious Parliamentarians captured a castle they blew it up. It was cheaper than putting in a garrison of their own, and it prevented the castle from being used by the enemy again. So gatehouses, keeps and curtain walls were always destroyed. Many old castles

The "slighting" of castles started in the Civil War and "the castle" as a way of life ended for ever more.

in isolated places had been abandoned by their owners because they were inconvenient, and these crumbled into ruins, but it was the Civil War that was responsible for the ruined state of most of the castles that we see today. After being "slighted" they lay open to wind and rain for centuries, and often their stones were plundered for local building.

A few castles were rebuilt and converted into great mansions, though they still look like castles. Warwick, Arundel, and Berkeley are among these. A few ultimately became prisons—Oxford, Chester, Lancaster, Lincoln, Exeter and Hereford. From the close of the 18th century it became fashionable for wealthy gentlemen to build vast mansions designed as castles. There was a great interest in the country's medieval past, and it was considered romantic to live in such houses. So there was a new crop of mock "castles". The most imposing of them is Penrhyn Castle in North Wales, with a "keep" said to be modelled on the famous keep of Rochester. The Victorians were even better at this kind of thing, and two of their "castles" are such realistic reproductions of a medieval fortress that you might well be deceived—Castell Coch, near Cardiff, and Peckforton Castle in Chester. Mock castles, however, aren't "real" castles, and only further illustrate the end of their era.